GW01417438

ARCHETYPAL GENDER

A new look at gender dysphoria in the light of a
case of transsexualism in multiple gender syndrome

by

Michael Anderton

I would like to dedicate this book to my wife Robin and my daughter Sophia for their constant support and to Oonah Ribet for her invaluable help with the editing.

Books may be ordered from 61 Brassey Road, Winchester SO22 6SB.

Price £9 plus p & p.

Printed by Sarsen Press, 22 Hyde Street, Winchester, SO23 7DR

CONTENTS

FOREWORD

I read the latest version of Michael Anderton's work when I was recently in Kandersteg, Switzerland, lamed by weak legs to necessarily waiting for my wife to return from a day's trek. I also read that day the International Herald Tribune of September 7, 2005 with its review of Ang Lee's new film *Brokeback Mountain*, made from a short story by Annie Proulx, about two young Wyoming cowboys who fall in love and one night live out their love which "in…bone-deep desire persists in the face of the most terrible taboo."

What I think Anderton does here is push farther than I have seen before, by a Jungian analyst, the psychological limits of valid erotic love. His is the kind of work that I like to see Jungians do; take weird case material from their patients and interpret it in unforeseen ways that are based upon what Anderton calls Jung's "seminal" concepts, far beyond where Jung himself, for whatever reason, took them. The reader can see that I am not a strict constructionist. Anderton's motivation is not only his being a somewhat revolutionary and restless analytic thinker but also his being a Christian priest, who found his patient supine on the streets of London. His movement out from the consulting room into the byways is reflected on his striking insistence on the necessity for a radical reappraisal of normalcy. I suspect that he moves that way because of his commitment to human redemption, as well as his need to stretch the parameters of conventional thinking. That need comes from heart.

Anderton obviously believes in the evolution of our understanding of psyche. His example encourages me and it will do the same for others.

Eugene Monick, M.Div., Ph.D.

5

BACKGROUND

"Shortly after we arrived in the house (and just married) there was a loud knock on the door. A rather drunken and slightly scruffy woman, who introduced herself as Kathleen, confronted us. Over the following weeks and months we got to know her better; she was well known in the area, was often drunk and noisy, and on occasions battered at our front door asking to see the vicar. She used to come in and talk, drink cups of tea with the odd sandwich (if she had no money to eat). She started to do odd jobs for the Church, and came to talk regularly to Michael. She was obviously an alcoholic and smoked too much, and suffered from ill health, so was unable to hold down a regular job. As far as family was concerned, she had an aunt in London somewhere and her beloved cat Bobo. Until the day she died her cards always sent love from her and Bobo, although the cat had died years before. When we left to live abroad five years later, she was still living as a woman although she was dressing more like a man and had cut her hair short, her handshake was always masculine. She kept in touch and told us that she had started to live as a man and call himself John, also that she had given up alcohol (she never drank again). When we returned to the UK four years later John had become fully male. He continued to see Michael for the rest of his all too short life. I visited him in hospital, in a male ward, a few days before he died of lung cancer. Although he was born female, his death certificate stated that he died as a male."

Robin Anderton

INTRODUCTION

The Bible is the tradition in which our whole view of relations in life, at least in our Western world, has grown, and is the root not only of our rational intellect but also of our feeling, intuition and symbolism. My frequent use of biblical language is essential in order to grasp and progressively understand the whole of the argument which is here set out. Psychological language alone without the use of biblical imagery cannot comprehend, physically and archetypally, the phenomenon of gender dysphoria. Therefore, a spectrum of biblical symbols should make it easier for the reader to find his or her way into the whole area which we are exploring, even though, from these premises, we shall be going on into the psychological, alchemical and philosophical aspects that have progressed out of the primary biblical revelation, and further towards a new symbolic picture in which our understanding is balanced and increased.

To begin with there is an underlying picture of the Genesis myth, where Adam and Eve in paradise, without sin and guilt, are ancestral symbols of primal humanity. Their subsequent Fall from grace and rebellion against the ultimate creator of origin with a loss of wholeness, is also a gain in potential with the emergence of the opposites as gods with the knowledge of good and evil and, therefore, with access to the Tree of Life.

At this stage there are two factors. Firstly, there is the descent of Mercurius, the personification of the opposites, as an agent of creation and a function of both the divine and human in the fall of mankind – the matrix of a redeeming principle in man as well as God. Secondly, there is the need of a redeeming principle for uniting the opposites in order to restore the original harmony and unity, and to take divided man, through an integrating transcendent symbol, into a re-creation partaking of the very Godhead itself. This mediatory symbol comes in the Christ event – the incarnation and crucifixion where, suspended between the opposites, the work of atonement (at-one-ment) is wrought. This Christ redeemer finds his complement in the Gnostic redeemer, Mercurius, forming the *lapis philosophorum* of alchemy and which, with the Christ, becomes the incarnation of the archetype of the God Man, or Anthropos, in which God and Man are united. Here is redemption for split and fallen man, and also for the split which God himself suffered in creating male and female, and in his fundamental unconsciousness where he seeks to become conscious in mankind.[1]

There is, perhaps, need to clarify also the psychological terms. The archetypes are the basic principle engrams underlying the whole of creation, mankind and the cosmos. They are separate in themselves but are experienced through the instincts in the body, where there is a transforming reaction as they are assimilated in the conscious ego, in symbol and image. They form the complexes, and are the gods – shadowy numinous figures connected in the Godhead to the ultimate archetype of God, as emanations of creation through Sophia Sapientia or divine wisdom.

As well as these multiple complexes, numinous in their manifestations, there are basic archetypes of male and female, mother and father, son and daughter, friend and enemy, brother and sister, king and queen, Adam and Eve, sun and moon, light and darkness, good and evil, as well as symbolic objects – minerals and metals, salt and sulphur (alchemically), the arcane substance of the *prima materia* of alchemy and orb and sceptre of rule and moral order, amongst others.

Animus and anima need some explanation. They are the contrasexual images of the male in the female, and the female in the male. These are primarily archetypally based symbols arising in the basic biological hermaphrodite, a part of the instincts and drives which we understand as eros. In the development of the soul in mankind through encounter with the Shadow, they become progressively psychological figures, numinous and partaking also of the spiritual. They are also uniting principles in divided and fallen mankind, and also part of evolution. Accelerated through the conflict of the opposites, and united in eros (biological love) and agape (spiritual love), they give birth to the divine child of the Self. The divine child grows assisted, by default, by the principle of evil – the raven, where suspended in crucifixion it becomes the Son of Man, the great hermaphrodite Self which is the mediaeval Christ; the one we all are, taking all things in the end of time into the Godhead. This we call the eschatological apotheosis.

The hermaphrodite is basic to our theme, and indeed to our lives as human beings. The individual is not only male and female biologically, but also psychologically in animus and anima. Gender dysphoria is where, in the male and female, bodily and psychological elements vary; male predominantly bodily and female psychologically, or female predominantly bodily and male psychologically. We must also remember that the male has breasts and a rudimentary vagina, and the female a clitoris or rudimentary penis. But in gender dysphoria we have a variation in the opposites which also has a basis in the normal hermaphrodite, where through creation and fall there is Mercurius. Mercurius, the god that became, in multiple opposites, an agent in creation and also in redemption in the union with the God Man, that is here an agent in evolution. Now we move from the physical biological to a new psychological archetypal nexus, where the soul becomes primary and fulfilled leading to spiritualization. The carrier of the new evolved hermaphrodite goes back to redeem the world, which is in bondage to a limited more physical tradition; a guilt ridden perversion of a true understanding with fear, and even partaking of, at this side of the grave, a living hell.

It is important to make clear in what sense the category of the Christ is to be understood. Acceptance of the historical figure of the Christ as Jesus of Nazareth is in no way to be understood in a doctrinaire way. Christ is to be seen as a presence throughout history from the beginning, in the present as an eternal 'now', and progressing towards the final consummation of all things. This presence is related to mankind in vision and dream, and as a fundamental principle in the creation and in the human personality as the true Self in the heart of every man. This is an existential experience in mankind as an archetype of the Self, as the mediator of the central experience of the evolving world psyche, and as the true hermaphrodite in which male and female are one in the individuated person.

The biblical, psychological and theological terms here take on a new perspective of meaning and lead us to a new age, where the transcendent symbols of greater understanding have yet to emerge. Here, fundamentally, is the archetype of marriage. The molecules of matter in the earth marry in binary and multiple form. The male and female also have multiple gender engrams where the symbol of marriage is a fundamental principle in the relationships of the race. However, psychologically the spectrum widens where the archetypal principle of marriage is a basic element in the encounter with multiple gender syndrome.

SYNOPSIS

1. There are multiple patterns of human relationships which are based on a ground plan of archetypal complexes.

2. These relationships are not eccentric and pathological but fundamentally normal.

3. They need to be reconciled to the guilt, fears, insecurities and marginalisation that surround all but the heterosexual norm, so that they can be seen to be acceptable in themselves, and so that both those involved and society are free to relate on every level, without competition, loss, betrayal, envy, jealousy or persecution.

4. Here we can postulate the need of humanity to progress beyond a severely moral and narrow cultural containing factor for the sexual mores in a developing society. The Christ himself postulates greater works and further revelation in the Spirit after his life on earth, which can also be seen in the philosophy and teachings of the Gnostics and Alchemists, and in the seminal contribution of C. G. Jung.

5. In this process of multiple relationships there is an inner as well as an outer factor. In the archetypal marriage of the opposites they meet in the hermaphrodite and syzigy of the hierosgamos, as part of the human and divine drama.

6. This is highlighted not only in the hermaphrodite nature of the normal person, but also in the transsexual gender-dysphoric.

7. In this book this theme is related to the experience and dreams of a transsexual gender-dysphoric, female to male with homosexual orientation.

LIST OF ILLUSTRATIONS

1. WHAT IS MULTIPLE GENDER?

Very little work has been published on Gender Dysphoria,[2] although there has been a certain amount of scientific research in terms of genetics and hormones, nurture and nature. The exposition of the following case may perhaps be a psychological and, to a certain extent, moral and theological contribution to this subject, that can perhaps throw light upon an archetypal situation more radical than the accepted nature and relationships of the male and the female.

The human race almost from the beginning appears to have based its case exclusively on male to female orientation, and a dual molecular marriage structure. The main theme of this book, following on the seminal contributions of C.G.Jung and others in Gnosticism and Alchemy, is working on the premise that underlying the creation is an archetypal groundswell, multiple and correlated, which emerges in the creation not only of opposites but in the many and various possible combinations of the male and female, and also of male to male and female to female. The fact of gender dysphoria opens up further combinations which, in their mercurial element of opposites throw more light on our theme. The female body with male sense of identity may have erotic transferences as normal male to female, or homosexual male to male. Correspondingly, the male biological body with female sense of identity may have erotic transferences as female to male, or lesbian female to female.

All this can be expressed diagrammatically where the following basic **Schema (1)** presents itself at this stage:

Erotic Transference

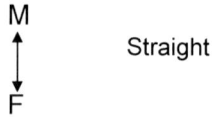

Straight

Homosexual

Lesbian

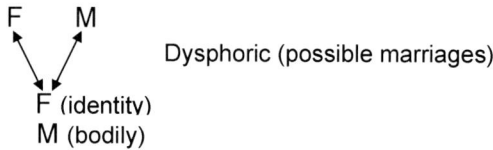

Dysphoric (possible marriages)

F (identity)
M (bodily)

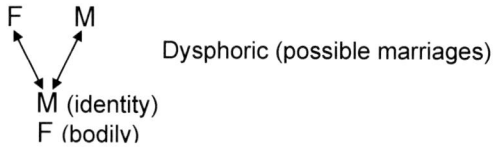

Dysphoric (possible marriages)

M (identity)
F (bodily)

This can take us so far, but there are other considerations that expand the understanding and projection of our theme, in particular that the human being is both naturally and psychologically hermaphrodite. This means that in each person as well as male and female complementary physical principles, where the male has breasts and a rudimentary vagina and the female, parallel to the penis, a clitoris, they have complementary male and female souls,[3] expressed as animus and anima.[4] Thus there is an inner female counterpart to the male – the anima, and an inner male counterpart to the female – the animus. These, because they are both archetypal and unconscious, cannot be defined too closely. In projection onto the opposite sex they can be of the nature of a bridge and empathetic relationship, but basically they are functions of oneself, one's other half, which can be integrated at least partially into the individual personality to form an inner marriage. It follows that in the human personality there are both biological and psychological elements, that is, the possibility for natural copulation with another, and an inner, archetypal conjunction.[5] Furthermore, beyond the purely natural or biological union with its outcome in the natural child, there is the archetypal marriage with the birth of the divine child. The natural child grows into the adult, and the divine child, who is attacked by the raven or negative principle for its progression, develops into the greater hermaphrodite, the Son of Man of Christianity or Mercurius, the Gnostic redeemer, in which the opposites are united. In one sense this is the one man or one woman that we all are. It follows, that if the individual finds a new wholeness in this way there exists the possibility of a relationship with another similarly integrated person, whether it be erotic or platonic, without being at the mercy of unconscious projection. This is similar to the individuation process of C. G. Jung which, although primarily inner, is also an outer relationship where the inner experience is lived out in life. Although we tend to see these as separate they are essentially parts of the same process.

The interesting thing is that both the homosexual and the lesbian have an animus and an anima, where each partner plays male-to-female and female-to-male roles, dominant or recessive, active or passive, which may be reflected in the genetic balance of their x and y chromosomes. This throws more light on the natural balances inherent in our multiple archetypal ground for all-male and all-female marriages, where there may also be the possibility of an inner marriage, all-male or all-female, inherent in the multiple gender syndrome.

For the gender dysphoric, moreover, whose underlying archetypal pattern of multiple gender orientation is more complex, the possibility of a similar spectrum of inner and outer marriages opens up. In other words, where we have a gender orientation between female to male in the body, as in our case history, there is also possible gender orientation of male to female or male to male, that has both animus and anima and the possibility of an inner marriage. Similarly, in male to female in the body, physically, there is the possibility of inner marriages of male to female and female to female. Therefore, in the light not only of outer marriages but also that of psychological and archetypal, i.e., animus and anima projections, we can enlarge our hypothesis in the form of **Schema 2** below:

Inner Marriage (soul)

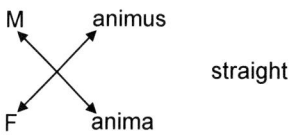

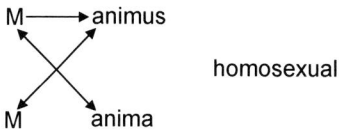

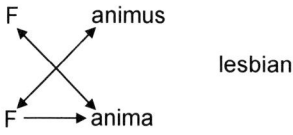

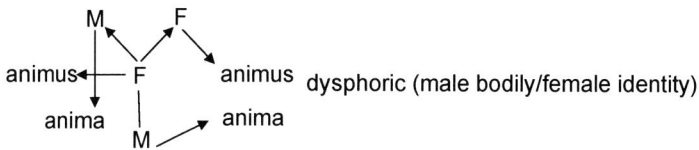

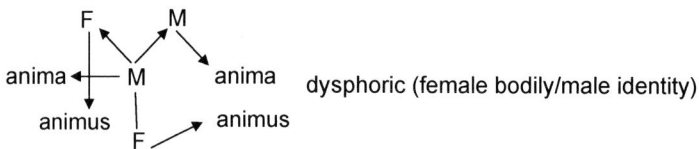

M   animus

straight

F   anima

M ⟶ animus

homosexual

M   anima

F   animus

lesbian

F ⟶ anima

M   F

animus ⟵ F   animus   dysphoric (male bodily/female identity)

anima   M   anima

F   M

anima ⟵ M   anima   dysphoric (female bodily/male identity)

animus   F   animus

To summarise and for reference in reading on we have the following picture:

1. Male-to-female straight (marriage) who project and then introject an animus and anima to incorporate the Self as an inner marriage.

2. Male-to-male homosexual (marriage) may have active and passive partners, who constellate animus and anima projections that introject as an inner marriage.

3. Similarly, female-to-female lesbian (marriage) may have active and passive partners, constellating animus and anima that introject as an inner marriage.

4. Female-to-male dysphoria, as in our case, can erotically relate male-to-female normal or male-to-male homoerotic, where there may be animus and anima projections, withdrawn to form an inner marriage.

5. Male-to-female dysphoria can erotically relate female-to-male normal, or female-to-female lesbian, where there may be animus and anima projections, withdrawn to form an inner marriage.

There are one or two points to make here. The constellation of the Self at one stage implies the divine child. Wherever we have a human being the child is potentially manifested both physically and psychologically. This occurs naturally in **1**, but in **2**, **3**, **4** and **5**, only physically through adoption or surrogate and other fertilisation techniques. In all cases the divine child stage can be psychological only. In the case where the gender dysphoric has a child through a normal male-female relationship, it must, for our purposes, be seen as dividing the life history into more than one separate stage (see Appendix I).

To understand the cultural implications of this argument we must follow the evolution of gender relationship norms throughout history. The initial male-female norms had to be preserved especially in a wandering unstable Jewish tribe to safeguard the continuity of the race, which crystallise in the commands of Moses, Christ and St. Paul. All imply that these are intermediate measures to preserve the status quo and the integrity of the social structure, and that there were other considerations that they were not ready to take on board at the time, and which in one sense we are not ready to take on board yet. But in the inner divine marriage of the Gnostics, Alchemists and Jung, we get an insight into the progression of the divine marriage, theologically known as the consummation of all things (at the end of time), where all are free to realise and fulfil the other without jealousy or loss.

Eros, especially in its feminine manifestations, is the relating function that breaks through the taboos and shibboleths of traditional legal morality into the freedom of the law of love. This is not for too much licence and abuse of freedom, but in order for transformation to happen.

This brings us to the question of the relationship between accepted normality and pathology, between healthy, natural and spiritual human nature, and between distortion and perversion of the true basic archetypal norms that stand beyond the existential conflict of the opposites, in all of which we live our mortal life. The orthodox doctrine states that the creation in the beginning was perfect but almost at once came the primal disobedience and the fall from grace. Thus the world seems to be a perversion from the original sound wholeness. It is arguable, however, that the dark side was present in God and mankind in paradise, even from the beginning, as an expression in its totality of the nature of God. Nevertheless, we must recognise that there are, even in normal sexual relationships, a neurosis, a guilt, and the possibility of some of the grossest perversions. These are also present in our homoerotic, molecular relationships, and in our hypothesis of the multiple gender relationships (see Appendix III). But this does not mean that they are unnatural in themselves, for they are part of the tapestry of infinite variety that we find in nature and in human relationships . We live in an ambivalent state between the opposites of matter and spirit, masculine and feminine, conscious and unconscious. The situation is mercurial, containing every combination of opposites, including the multiplicity of our various gender complexes. Here is the archetypal beginning and the end, where God and man or woman together evolve in our world cosmic continuum of time and space.

In our case both in dream and actual experience we can see the nature of these multiple, erotic experiences with all their potential, both natural and symbolic, in a living experience. Here we encounter the possibility of its greater development in all its richness.

After this introductory preamble we are now in a position to follow, illustrate, and amplify our argument through the analysis and experience of a male, born anatomically female, yet masculine primarily of soul, i.e. animus, with homosexual orientation to the male.

2. LIFE HISTORY OF JOHNNY BLUE

John, J'ai, ----------- known as Johnny Blue, was a transsexual female to male, with homosexual orientation. His analysis with me began after I found him dying in a street market of cirrhosis of the liver some twenty years ago. He came off alcohol, and had an operation for the removal of his gall bladder, and the reduction of an enlarged omentum. He nearly died under the anaesthetic. He was brought up of Irish Catholic parents and realised, through traumatic bullying at school, that although he was physically female his soul and gender orientation was predominantly male. It was obvious that the whole personality was highly masculine, the hormone levels were male, not female. He was increasingly repulsed at the thought of female penetration, often felt that he had a phantom phallus, and was the aggressive partner in male to male sexuality. He gathered round him a circle of transsexual and gay friends and had as a passive lover a university lecturer, which was a relationship both tender and almost violent in forceful use of the prosthesis. He relates how progressively he came to hate the feminine, and tells the story of an apparition he had in his mother's kitchen which was undoubtedly possessed in part by occult phenomena including a strange wraith-like homunculus, which did all sorts of mercurial antics towards him and seemed to mock his gender dysphoria.

He had a familiar who was a presence which had an animus aura to him, called J'ai (Fig.1), with whom he identified. Also, far more real than mere fan adulation, he had a *participation mystique* with an actor as a sort of soul mate. When they were younger they were almost physically identical in appearance. He had had many occult experiences in which, uninvited and unrecorded, the voice of J'ai appeared on tapes accompanied by strange music and sounds. He also had synchronistic experiences, with the actor's agent sending him

Figure 1.   J'ai. Jonnie Blue's familiar

tapes and literature. He had a remarkable talent combining music, drama, poetic literature and art, but there had never been an opening for it other than in the very grass roots of life. The college doors never opened. When he was a youth he had a dream, in which he went up to the door of a music college which had a large knocker; he knocked, the knocker fell off, and the door never opened.

He had an unsuccessful operation for gender orientation, and a hernia developed in the abdomen. Heavy smoking had caused a condition of the lungs which made anaesthetic dangerous and which, together with the difficult hernia itself, resulted in an inoperable condition. At the depth of depression after this diagnosis, with talk of suicide going over the brink of sanity, the actor came to perform in London. He went to see him act and at the stage door afterwards there was a remarkable meeting. The actor left most of his audience and talked to John for a good half hour alone, asked to see his pictures, and remained in contact. It was almost as if there was a very special relationship from the beginning, even before birth. He came out of his depression and began to paint again, and recorded some dreams in the next few weeks which interpret the very central themes of our hypothesis. His Catholic background persecuted him, and sometimes he needed great assurance where he felt under the displeasure and judgement of God, fearing hell and eternal damnation. One dream showed the diseased and sin-bearing Christ healing and accepting, and the young actor as the positive brother and as a Christ figure, forgiving as opposed to the antagonistic accuser. He said he could never commit suicide. The threat was to go over the edge of sanity.

As we shall see, these dreams are highly redeeming. Whilst acknowledging the true nature of his gender dysphoria, the balance of his masculinity still needed the feminine, the anima, to balance and make for a true and wholesome masculinity in the whole personality. We see this happening in the dreams where interpretation reveals a revolution of accepted attitudes, compensation, and the dynamic of an enantiodromia.[6] It comes in the darkest hellholes, when he paints urinals as gothic cathedrals; a true transformative holiness in the excrement of life, where the inferior function in the Shadow is reconciled and the evil assimilated. Amongst his many symbols was a power station which generated intense masculine and feminine energy, overshadowed by the 'horses of the apocalypse' (see p.26). He had a strange, almost shamanistic, affiliation with animals. (In alchemy it says that those who are kind to animals succeed in the work.) The hernia still blew out like a great balloon which felt to him like a sort of phantom pregnancy. This, symbolically, is where the divine child of the soul, the transformation of his personality, sought to be born. As we worked with his dreams which were both personal and collective, he came to realise that these experiences had a meaning beyond the everyday – meaning and value for his inner life with its expression in outer reality.

3. THE STORY OF THE DREAMS

On the whole we will let the dream and analytical material speak for themselves, as we feel this would be more authentic. Interpretation will follow each dream, together with its relation to the psychological and empirical world in which we live. Bearing this in mind, the following themes are those which will be stressed:

1. The relation of the masculine and feminine gender archetypes and symbolic images to the balance of a sound and stable masculinity, in itself in relation to the female as subsidiary to the male.

2. The role of the contra sexual principles of animus and anima in this.

3. The healing of the sexual orientation in the male to female and female to male, in consummation on a psychological and spiritual level, also in the male to male and the female to female. (Note the appearance of a virginal priestly figure and the presence of the Christ, in assurance of acceptable creative activity.)

4. The fear of guilt and the judgment of God allayed by the assuring presence of the forgiving Christ, with a positive way forward.

5. The release of creative activity and the freedom to fulfil inborn talent through an opening in a relationship, which is both psychological and actual.

6. The assurance from the Christ that John's multiple gender orientation has a normal and natural basis. Furthermore, that it should be accepted

and lived as a contribution in our world to an increased and deepened understanding of archetypal sexuality, and the multiple roles of a changing genotype as an evolutionary process.

DREAM 1

In my flat in the bedroom. A very tall big woman, about ten feet in height, was having a go at me over my dirty windows. I was reduced in height to about two feet tall. I felt diminished. Everything seemed huge. This bloody woman kept going on and on at me, and I was getting smaller. Suddenly there was a loud bang and the woman disappeared. I grew back to my normal height but felt inwardly diminished. I sat on my bed and was crying, and when I looked my tears were blood, not water. Suddenly it seemed as if the room was awash with bloody tears. The phone rang in the distance and I woke up.

Here we see the encounter with the feminine in the Shadow. As is often found in homosexuals, this woman appears very large and he very small. She rebukes him and threatens him continually. His windows are dirty – his outlook on life is not clear. Suddenly there is an orgasmic bang. Here is the beginning of a reconciling healing of the position. He comes to his normal size and yet cries tears of blood, perhaps of remorse, self-pity and sorrow, but surely of the menstrual fluid of the female in him awash as the Shadow unconscious threatens to possess him. Then the phone in the distance, the contact with normal reality, wakes him up and brings him back to safety after the operation of the dream.

The way to heal the neurosis is through it, not away from it. The dream makes him face the situation of the enormous Shadow of the feminine. The following dream does this even more explicitly:

DREAM 2

Looking in hall mirror trying on a baseball cap. Suddenly this female entity appeared by a front door and said 'there you go causing trouble again'. Then a creature with long silky fur appeared in my sitting room, a cross between a big dog and an anteater. It grabbed my thumb and started to suck it, drawing down its long proboscis. I pulled my thumb back quick. Then there was a long thin piece of transparent pink plastic on the table. I went to pick it up. It turned on me attacking me. It seemed to have suddenly grown teeth and was trying to bite me. I grabbed it, and sawed it off the wall. Then over in the corner I have a stack of shelves, and as I looked, somehow this big armchair, which I have not got, seemed to have attached itself to the top two shelves, and the whore was sitting in it looking down at me contemptuously, and told me to remove the pile of paper from under the chair. Then over by the other wall, which seemed to stick out with a door in the side of it, was a table with eating forks upon it. This other woman appeared and demanded I give her thirty-one forks. She grabbed the forks, putting them in a plastic bag, then disappeared in the door in the side of the wall. There was a man in the wall who said, 'thank you very much'. I said, 'give me back my forks'. The door was shut on me. Then I opened the door, which was my bedroom, and I got an awful sensation of fear and let out a scream. And then I woke up.

He is looking at his image in the mirror, as it were in the vestibule of the hall, trying on a baseball cap. The baseball represents 'base' masculinity, and also experimentality in transgender and homosexuality. The 'creature' is the basic instinctive life sucking at his thumb, a symbol of his active power, and the anteater's proboscis is drawing in and eating up his ability to earn his meat and daily bread in life. Pink plastic is for the despised feminine girl in him that develops a negative aspect – a *vagina dentata* – that attacks him, which he then isolates so that it becomes an autonomous complex. The shelves, the chair and the papers represent a collective affinity to the household of living. The pile of paper, or papers of work, that the whore exposes as mere paper – a hollow persona – is his attitude to society. The woman demands the forks, a symbol of the trickster-devil that he needs so badly in order to stand up against the establishment, and to establish his own nature, work and identity both in his gender orientation and as a creative artist. Three and one (31 forks) – numbers of the masculine trinity and the Godhead – are numinous numbers of his true masculinity. He gives them over and the door is shut. He is marginalized and shut in with an awful primal scream. He is being denied his identity as a real person and the realisation of his creative talent, both of which are essential to a developing sense of salvation.

To understand this dream one needs to know that in terms of life he had a very ambivalent relationship with the established order – work and career, conformity with the powers that be, and employment. He was of the generation of the alternative society that opted out and did its own thing. This called down upon itself the approbation and demands of the superego, particularly here of the mother, not only for the gender dysphoria trouble, but also for not conforming to the collective ideals of life, conduct, and style. Represented here is the Shadow of the Great Mother – the archetypal mother – who had been rejected and now had to be faced.

We return now to the incorporation of the feminine, where his attitudes to society are a reflection of the projections of the Great Mother.

DREAM 3

I appeared to be in the Barbican Centre. Then I was running up some steps outside, which don't exist. This man was chasing me asking me back for his jumper, which I did not know I was wearing till I looked at my chest. Then there was this glass cabinet down beside the stairs, with compartments of various sizes going into the middle, all with glass doors. I had to get this blue bottle, with blue aftershave, that was locked in the middle compartment at the end of a small square tunnel of glass doors. Then I was in this place, all wet and muddy, and there were broken corrugated iron fences. To the left was a corrugated iron structure, which was a urinal, with a lot of little boys shitting and pissing and having fun. Then I was drawn in, but was pushed by an invisible force down this middle path which was all muddy and wet. To the right was this single piece of corrugated iron, which this dilapidated old urinal was hanging off, and this solitary little boy in rags who was pissing at it. I walked past him, he never looked up. Then I was aware of hiding behind this corrugated iron fence, under this dead bush, and it was all mud and wet on the ground. I tried to cover myself with old paper that was lying around. I had a feeling I was being chased, but it was not me the military were looking for. There was this man on the other side of the waste ground. He had black curly hair and a thick beard. He looked Latin and his name was Andrew. He was a guerrilla fighter. Then I was in this car. This other man was driving. Then he disappeared and this Latin woman was driving it. Next to her was this beautiful boy, jet-black hair, dark tanned skin and very dark eyes. I said to him 'give me a fag mate'. The woman said to the boy, 'give the gentleman a cigarette'. He took two cigarettes from his top pocket, handed me one, lit one for me, and then lit one for himself. He never looked at me, he just looked straight ahead. Then this other man appeared somewhere else, not in the car, the car had vanished and there was the other woman, who appeared to be Latin. The man said to her, pointing to another woman, 'she's Jewish'. The Latin woman asked her name. The Jewish woman said it was ELENA. They were both very beautiful. They could not see me; it was as if I was invisible, bodiless. The Latin woman was the leader of a guerrilla movement. She took this Jewish woman to a small room and went to bed with her. I appeared to be watching this, as if I were in suspended animation, looking down at them. Then I woke up.

The scene is the Barbican – a higher-class level – where we get a jumping up the social level. He is wearing the jumper without realising it until he looks at his chest with its female breasts, where the gender dysphoric is put down in society. The tension between these two creates the integration of the male and female in his personality.   But he is in the glass cabinet. This is the glass cabinet in which Morgan le Fé bewitched Arthur and Merlin, and where the green lion of alchemy swallows the glass stone charm and is bewitched by the feminine,[7] where he finds his bottle of blue aftershave. Blue is the colour of the masculine, electric, elemental spirit and also, incidentally, the colour of the Blessed Virgin Mary. Through the centering of the doors – the middle compartment of the psyche, and the quaternary of the square tunnel – the wholeness of the personality in the four functions of the ego, there seems to be a coniunctio and union of the masculine and feminine principles. Here there is a wholeness of the personality in body and psyche.

Then he takes his place as a little boy amongst the shit in the rough area of corrugated iron, i.e., the men of iron of the working classes in Plato's The Republic. He is pushed down the 'middle path' of double gender, and marginalized and isolated in society. He covers himself with old paper – the conventional persona, the false establishment, and realises in himself archetypal principles – the very manly guerrilla/the beautiful boy, and meets the anima in various guises. Here the redeeming principle of the archetypes is becoming manifest – multiple images or complexes from the unconscious for the realisation in consciousness of the higher personality.

Greater and more powerful collective images are the Latin woman (Roman civilisation), and the Jewish woman (religious consciousness of the Jewish genius of law and judgement, mercy and salvation), both images of the anima. ELENA is a mixture of Helen of Troy of the light, and Lilith/hell signifying darkness. These dual goddesses combine high feminine love to love him, which love he in turn has to incorporate and reciprocate.

We have here the basic scene of his relationship of the feminine, the anima, to life itself, and the redemption of his fixed and hardened unbalanced attitudes, in order for him both to come to himself as a child and to integrate a sound maleness as a sexually gay man. We also look to the fruits of that redemption – the healing of his guilt through the acceptance of his fellow man as soul mate, and the seal set on this by the Christ the mediator (see next dream).

DREAM 4

I was walking along this very narrow ledge on this very high building. All these mocking voices were calling 'go on fall off you bastard, why do you not jump?'. In this dream I had the hernia, which had bloated to an enormous size, and was getting bigger and bigger, gradually pulling me onto a narrow ledge. The voices kept shouting, 'bloat, bigger, bloat. Go on jump you grotesque bastard.' Then the sky went very dark and the crucifixion appeared. The Christ showed me my suffering in him. He appeared very lonely with a hugely distended abdomen. He looked at me and his eyes were full of tears. He had my eyes; he felt my pain physically and mentally. Then the vision vanished. I was right on the edge and I was ready to jump, when I looked down on the city of broken dreams. I saw my art, my music, my life smashed against a rock. I was bereft of feeling. I could see my blood running down the channel of an old urinal. That is it, now for it, I have had enough. As I went to jump I was pulled upwards by my arms. I felt calmer, the voices were still shouting at me. I was hauled off the ledge and dropped gently on warm sand. When I looked around the actor soul mate was sitting next to me on the sand. He said 'I heard you and I came. You must live, as you are important to life, and I love you. Your body is not you, you are higher than it, we are here in the life a short time. Your soul is forever, you body is not.' I said 'did you see the vision?'. He said 'yes, I was sleeping and I saw everything. My body is asleep in bed, I am here with you, your body is asleep in your flat. This is the astral realm, J'ai. You and I are inseparable, we do not need bodies here. See how blue everything is now, you have rescued me before now and I come to you to help you. Christ feels all our suffering, we are never alone, and because we were together before time, so shall it be until the end of time.' I said embracing him, 'I love you. But I am being pulled back, I do not want to go back.' He said 'you must, your work is not yet finished.' I said 'what work?, I have nothing to offer the world'. He said, 'J'ai, you are so wrong, you have given of yourself. We both must go back to our bodies, we will wake soon, we will come together again. Your hernia is a cross you have to bear, having a beautiful body is not everything, if you could see yourself as I see you, you would know what I mean.' We embraced, then he vanishes, and I woke up bloated as hell but calm, very calm, and very warm feelings surrounding me.

He is walking along a high and narrow ledge where he is to be tested between hubris and despair. The devils are shouting and mocking, a parallel to Christ's temptations, but they are his own as a human being, where the judgement of his hernia becomes bigger and bigger. There is a union of the Christ Self. The Christ, who identified with his sufferings and bore the disease and sin of the world, is but a reflection of himself. In Christ they are one, sharing the responsibility. Then the Christ disappears; each man alone must make his own unique response and carry his own responsibility. He is tempted to jump in suicide but the angels prevent him and lift him up, the voices are all shouting around. Faust is delivered even if he seems to have sold his soul to the devil. Then the Christ reappears in the face of his soul mate, his fellow man. He lands on the warm sand, symbolising the gentle leaven of the feminine, the earth by the waters of life, the mercy of the virgin and here, also, the wisdom and sharing of his soul-mate alter ego, where his brother man comforts and teaches him, making him more conscious of the reality of the situation, physically and spiritually, in time and in eternity. Sealed in brotherly love in the blue of the *coniunctio* of masculine and feminine, the dichotomy of body and soul, matter and spirit is expounded and resolved. There then follows a return to the world where the work is to be fulfilled. He nestles in the calming womb of the earth having to accept his cross of suffering, but with the grace to do so and to overcome.

The following dream is the climax to which all this has been leading. In one sense it is an apotheosis in which the soul lives out, in psychic action, the redeeming symbols.

DREAM 5
The actor soul mate appeared to me dressed all in white. His gaze transfixed me with love, authority, power and awe, and we stood before each other equal. We then had intercourse in ecstatic bliss. Firstly him as male and myself as female, in full vaginal penetration and orgasm. Then myself as male and him as female, followed by myself as male and him as the male partner, in full conjunction anally and in orgasm. Then as we stood and embraced the Christ appeared as a great high priest, magnificently robed and of great authority. He said 'be assured, this is the seal of divine approval on mutual multiple sexuality, and your own multiple gender orientation in particular. This is for all men and women to know and realise, where in it the guilt of the curse on the world is redeemed, and the archetypes manifest in their pristine origin and evolve to their true glory.' Then there appeared three shadow priest figures.

The actor, robed in white, is exercising the priestly function of the virgin soulmate. The Christ and the unseen visitors in the shadow together manifest a redemption on every level, Mercurial, human and divine, and in the shadow the archetypal gods meet in the light of the Christ. In the situation there is a realization of the greater humanity in the work of illumination of the true consciousness.

The dream is overwhelming and powerful and tells its own story of vindication of the curse of mankind, the apotheosis of redeeming transformation and the beginning and end, in which both simple and complex opposites are united and true basic reality revealed. But our story doesn't end here. It is still going on. The work is to be manifest on earth, and the analysis of the whole man, which we shall explore, is to be completed.

DREAM 6
Me and the actor standing amongst the ruins of a building. He was wearing an open, white, well-worn denim shirt, showing his bare chest. His nipples were pierced and he had a gold ring in each one, and a silver earring in

his right ear. He was wearing black leather jeans and he had a padlock and chain around his neck He reached out to me and put a padlock and chain around my neck. I was a complete male and taller than him and I was wearing a ribbed white shirt and ribbed jeans. I had body markings and tattoos and was very horny. I embraced him and ejaculated and then woke up.

The Christ has disappeared and he and the actor are alone amongst the ruins, symbolising the break-up of the old for the new to emerge. There is the appearance of the true hermaphrodite, male and female, adorned with the gold of the lapis, the *elixir vitae* of alchemy. The white denim shirt is practical sanctity, and the black jeans, hells angels, the dark side of God. Here the true masculinity of John rises in his own task, in his totality, serving God in his world in his own right. This, as we shall see from later dreams, is his initiation into a priestly role in the service of suffering humanity – the consummation of the hermaphrodite into the new being, the higher Self.

4. THE COURSE OF THE ANALYSIS

To round out the picture we shall take a look at, and follow, the course of the analysis as it affects the whole life picture.

The first stage was the physical and mental recovery where, in the very depths of life, he was dying (see p.24). The alcoholism gradually got better as we examined his relationship with the very maw of the earth, which is the domain of the Great Mother[8] (Dreams 2,3,4,5). The curse of the family, society, and the establishment left him rebellious and morbid to his life force, where the liver in alcoholism was practically destroyed by an advanced condition of cirrhosis. We found him not making any effort at employment, indeed really unfit to work, and in trouble with the Department of Health and Social Security. In addition he had problems with housing, was short of money, not feeding himself properly, and feeling intense social and religious guilt over his gender orientation, where not only the feminine physical characteristics but also a grossly enlarged stomach omentum made it difficult to appear in public, or exercise in the gymnasium. Nor was there any outlet for creative activity, which in the depth of his condition was, nevertheless, burning inside him. He eventually dried out, but the condition of his liver was so advanced that he had to have an operation for the removal of the gall bladder. At this time also the omentum was reduced. He nearly died after the operation, but then things began to improve. Social Security and housing were sorted out, and he was able to work for a gramophone company for a bit and do some gardening and building-site work. But his ability to work did not last. Psychologically it was a matter of motivation, his heart was not in it. The rebellious anarchist and the artistic temperament in him could not conform. He was able to find some encouragement in the courses on art, music and drama offered by the council, and got help with grants for materials from local charities. There was a degree of latent genius in which he combined writing poetry, drama and music in theatrical combination, and also began painting on a symbolic level. Somehow the curse of the shut door of the music college seemed to follow him, and there was always something preventing him getting his work off the ground. There emerge two main factors that show the direction of his development, which are at the core of the analysis.

Firstly, there was the realisation of the creative principle. He saw the actor we have mentioned on the television, and there was instant rapport. He felt that they had always known each other, even before the beginning of time. The physical resemblance was quite remarkable, and there was something far greater and deeper than mere fan adulation – a soul mate, a *participation mystique* that was almost tangible, and a communion of soul in which he felt, in psychological telepathic communication, that they were mutually helping each other. He went to see him but only amongst the crowd, for several years. He communicated with the actor's agent who sent him tapes and recordings. These assisted his mutual meditations in active imagination which were often of a highly erotic nature. He felt guilt. Was he doing harm? But together we realised that they were giving each other of the life force, which the dreams show (Dreams 4,5,6,7). There were occult experiences such as, the day before a tape would arrive in the post, although not known beforehand the exact name of the recording would come into his mind. His familiar, J'ai, was an intermediary, and we dealt with the relationship as an alter ego and an animus figure that was a mediator of his fundamental myth in the individuation process. There was an underlying feeling and distant hope that one day they would meet, but which began to fade into the background.

Secondly, there was the failure of the transsexual operation and the inoperable hernia which could not help being infiltrated with guilt and fear of judgement, as was the alcoholism, with the transsexulism and homosexuality seen as a perversion unacceptable in society.

In the depths of despair and on the borderline of sanity, he went to see the actor on stage. In the green room afterwards there was a remarkable meeting where everyone else seemed to disappear and go their own way, and they talked for at least half an hour and embraced as if they had known each other forever. The actor asked to see his art, and continued to communicate encouraging him. These meetings catalysed something that seemed perpetually alive. They wrote to each other and talked not only about art but also about their deepest aspirations, where they recognised their mutual participation and the help mutually given, in psyche and in spirit. (They did not have a sexual relationship except in J'ai's dreams.) Evidence of this is in the dreams. There is the immensely significant one for our hypothesis (Dream 5) that we have already quoted, but there are also others that show an immense healing and liberation of soul, a redemption from guilt and judgement, and the bursting forth of artistic talent. In dreams he and the actor were together. He was very depressed and could see no opening for his talent, and he was on the verge of suicide and giving up. The actor said (Dreams 4,5,6), 'we both have talent, and you have so much to give to the world of art, of music, of drama, of poetry. All that you have been through is but a preparation for what all of us together, as true hermaphrodites, male and female and multiple gender being, have to give to the world. Take courage, we will help each other and go out and forward to overcome.' This is a constant theme in the psychological relationship with the actor and bore fruit in many pictures, some of which we will illustrate as we go along.

He had for many years had a relationship with the Bankside power station before it became the Tate Modern art gallery (Dream 7 below). He felt drawn to it with a sort of electric magnetism which, in his paintings, was of a metallic blue colour, the colour of the masculine elemental spirits of the universe, and also feminine as the colour of the Blessed Virgin Mary. Here he experienced a mystic *coniunctio* and took on another name, Johnny Blue. He painted this, drawn towards it again and again both actually and symbolically. It represents a sort of apotheosis, a consummation of talent connected eschatologically with the horses of the apocalypse – an image of male and female instinctive energy driving into the end of time.

DREAM 7

The Bankside power station before it became the new Tate Modern gallery. The Power station was not on the Thames, it was on the edge of a blue sea, it was built out of deep blue glass. The sun and moon were a metallic blue set in a dark blue sky; they were both in the sky together at the same time. The sand was blue; it was warm all the time. The actor and me were dancing together on the sand. We were both younger, in the 30's, dancing to trance music and love songs which came from the ether coming from the power station. I was complete male. We lay down on the sand and made love. Then swam together in the blue sea. As we came out of the sea this figure, the Great Hermaphrodite, was standing on the shore. They beckoned us. We went over to them. They said 'you are our children. We are well pleased with our sons; you love each other, that is good. When you make love, you please us with your virility. Your children are your art, music, drama, dance. Your skins are a deep metallic blue, the colour of the caelum, creative male spirits of the universe, they are your brothers. Your lovemaking brings them to you, they inspire you, you inspire each other. Now we bless your union, go and create your art to our honour. But firstly to the honour of the vast one, the creator who lives in the void.' They blessed us, and we entered the power station and were prolific in our creations - art, music, drama. Making love a complete unity of two. And then I woke up.

This part of the analysis comes together in the following long and intense dream.

Michael is the name of the analyst.

DREAM 8

J'ai (me) was walking through the rubble of the City and the West End. He, (I) went to where the theatre was. It was still standing, only just though. I went through what used to be the stage door, down some winding steep steps, and found the actor's dressing room; the door was on the floor, the walls caved in. J'ai paused, where is the actor? I found what was left of the stage. Here he is, thank God. I ran up to him, he had been crying. I picked him up and carried him out of the theatre, and ran with him in my arms to what was Leicester Square Underground. I found myself running; carrying him along the tracks, through the tunnel for what seemed like miles, then towards the side of the tunnel there was an alcove. A man was sitting on an armchair. He had a candle on a table. He said, 'stop and sit down'. The man seemed to be in the shadow. I could make out his features. It was Michael. Oh thank Christ, I thought. I put the actor under a chair then I sat down. Michael gave us both some fresh water and a little food. Michael said, 'after you have rested I will guide you both out of here. In some parts of this harbour you are not safe. I have been waiting for you both.' The actor was clinging to me. I told him not to be afraid. Michael stood up and put his hands on our heads and said a prayer in a strange language. After our rest, Michael took the candle and said, 'follow me'. We both walked behind Michael through the tunnel. I could feel the actor's hand gripping mine. We carried on for what seemed an eternity, and then Michael said 'this is where you will both be safe'. We said, 'where are we?'. Michael said, 'this is the edge of time and space, this is the void'. I said, 'are you coming with us Michael?'. He said 'no, there are many others, I must go back and wait for them. I still have work to do'. The actor said, 'what happened?'. Michael said, 'in the end is the beginning and the beginning the end'. I said, 'are we alive?'. Michael said, 'yes. Now go and remember it is a continuum. As above so below. You will always be together.' Then the actor and I put our arms around each other's waist and watched Michael as he went back into the tunnel. Then I was woken up by an explosion, a car backfired in the street. I was in a trance all day after the dream, everything here seemed unreal – the roads, the traffic, even the cup of coffee I was drinking. It was like none of this so-called reality except for one thing, to gain experience. I looked at the actor's photo and smiled, and then got on with the rest of the day.

It seems as if they are in danger on the physical level of time and space. People will not understand. The man in the street will backfire on their sacred treasures, and they must move into the eternal timelessness of the unconscious, with its own dimensions and its own laws. The experience they are carrying is dangerous on the human bodily level, where it partakes of much existential conflict and misunderstanding in the collective. But in psyche and spirit it will authenticate itself in them, and bring the ship safely to harbour and the fruit to perfection.

5. THE INDIVIDUAL AND COLLECTIVE MYTH

It would seem apposite here to say something about the individual and collective myth, in relation to the realisation of creative talent and personal identity in society. This is not a simple singular factor, but has multiple progressive dimensions and an evolution on different levels.

The embryo contains, latent within itself, all that it is and all that it needs of knowledge and skill. It is likened to the acorn in which the potential growth of the mature oak tree is all contained. This embryo contains the whole destiny and fate of the individual, the outgrowth of its own unique nature which we shall call the individual myth. This is intimately connected to the myth of all other beings in the groundswell of creation. In one sense these contaminate each other as a *massa confusa*. This is the origin of the Collective Unconscious as a universal collective. This is the original state in paradise, relative unconsciousness in dreaming innocence. At the onset of the fall from grace there is a division of the original wholeness, when the cohesive vision and direction of the original myth is broken up. Ignorance and lack of skills enter in with the loss of innate wisdom, and the relationships that are contained in the instincts become distorted and severed from one another, in alienation and isolation.[9] But there is a potential gain as the opposites open up with the promise of a higher consciousness, as 'god(s) knowing good and evil'.[10] It is a place of conflict, 'a mild evil and a sweet wound'[11] at its best, and humankind is condemned to hard labour, eating bread by the sweat of the brow.[12] This calls for a redeeming symbol to unite the opposites which, when it is effective, not only restores the basic archetypal nexus as found in paradise, but takes the situation onto a higher level. On this higher level, partaking of the very nature of the gods in the Godhead, and through the archetypes, there is an incarnation as god-men and god-women with a greater stature and an enhanced individual and collective myth.[13] The purpose of this myth is the evolution of humankind on every level of the personality. The supreme redeeming symbol is the cross, its horizontal limbs uniting mankind in the world, and its vertical dimension uniting heaven, earth and hell. Here on the cross is the Christ, the saviour of the microcosm and the macrocosm, uniting the opposites in a transcendent symbol. But notice it does not remain static there, but translates from doctrines of sacrifice and baptisms from dead works – the Pauline 'milk unto babes' – to the weightier matters of the law, righteousness and judgement, and the fulfilment of the individual and collective destiny. The law here is not the law of the Ten Commandments, but the judgement is as to whether each person and each society have fulfilled their myths in terms of an evolving process to its fulfilment for man and god at the end of time. This is a theatre of mankind and the gods, vitally alive in the service of the living God, a process in which the world is evolving in individual creative responsibility, collectively reciprocating and dovetailing within each individual myth in the collective, to create a universal myth. This depends on each one redeeming and fulfilling an inborn and re-created talent, which is essential to personal and collective salvation.

6. TRANSFORMATION

We have seen how the oppression of society, guilt and fear threw John into the very grass-roots of existence, as when the knocker coming off the door of the music college blocked him from getting into life successfully in any way (see p.24). At this stage in the analysis he developed a compulsive obsession with urinals, which he painted over and over again. There is a progression in the paintings with the appearance of great gothic cathedral windows above the urinals, making a sacred shrine (Fig.2). Note how the pillar in the centre of the urinals emerges as a great phallus-lingam out of the yoni, as the vessel at the base. It is as if, in the primal place of excrement there is a sort of release akin to repentance, where the defilement of the soul is purged in physical symbolism. There is a complex reaction right down at the bottom of existence, where the Mercurial element in the gender dysphoria is set in a place of evolving transformation. Gradually he moves to a psychological level above the basic shit, as the urinals become baroque and glorious, made of fine gold – the transforming gold of the *lapis*, the philosophers' stone (Fig.3). Here he feels himself to be wholly male.

The next painting, an apotheosis of the urinal experience (Fig.4), shows a large crucifix with an entwining serpent. The serpent is like the serpent of evil, which the Christ bears on the cross for its transformation into wisdom.[14] Contained beneath the cross are the urinals, now much smaller. Standing on the arms of the cross are male and female hermaphroditic figures, with sun, moon and other *coniunctio* symbols. We can see here how the true personality emerges in the archetypal union of the opposites. There follows a picture of the sacrifice of the phallus (Fig.5). The steps lead out of the urinals of the basic physical male, ascend through a *puer aeternus* in the agony and ecstasy of orgasm, to the mature erect phallus entering the *caelum* or transcendent space – the vortex of sun and moon – into its highest self. In the

Figure 2. The temple of the urinals as a gothic shrine with the sacred phallic pillar and fire

Figure 3. Transformation of the urinal shrine into the alchemical gold altar of the lapis

following two dreams we can see that there has been a gradual progression from the grass roots to a more integrated level.

DREAM 9
Large building like an Egyptian temple, built from large white tiles. I entered in and there was a large circular cage with bars around it. There was a man in a wheel chair; he did not see me through the bars. There was a pigeon standing next to him. Then there was this narrow winding staircase. I went up the stairs; there was a huge book open. Both pages had moving colours like the colours in oil, and the writing on the bottom of the pages said 'city of tourmaline'. I felt a presence behind me and was told telepathically not to look back behind me.

He comes out of the white tiles of the urinals to an Egyptian temple, symbolically a sacralisation of the fleshpots of Egypt.[15] He is caged and still crippled, and

Figure 4. The apotheosis of the urinal experience through the altar of sacrifice with the crucifixion and serpent and a new wholeness, completed in the hermaphrodite androgynous pair of the coniunctio and inner marriage

Figure 5. The sacrifice of the phallus in transformation. An ascent from the depths in the realisation of the Self

Figure 6. Doubled with the male brother, Johnny Blue as the complete male, with the 'J' of his name on a gold pendant around the neck

Figure 7. The two brothers: a coniunctio drama of John with the alter ego, actor, soul mate as pair of lovers in the harmony of bliss

a bird symbolising the spiritualization of the instincts promises relief. Up the stairs, the spiral of process in time, is the book of life in Mercurial colours of the redemptive process.[16] It is sealed in tourmaline, the healing mineral of the integration of the organic flesh and one of his own healing stones. He is now to go forward and not look back, although there is a shadow behind him. He has work to do.

DREAM 10
Another urinal with gothic stained glass windows. Very old high urinals, with the usual white narrow tiles, all stained with age. The gothic stained glass windows were over the urinals. I had to get on a high step to the urinals; there was no roof, just dark grey bluish sky. I stood there and looked down on myself. I was complete male. I was tall and muscular and angular, and was naked except for a blue letter 'J' which was on a thick gold chain around my neck (Fig. 6). I was totally alone, there was music coming from the ether around, it was trance music. I seemed to be waiting for something. The music got louder. This small boy appeared next to me, he had deep auburn hair and deep brown eyes; he smiled up at me then disappeared. I felt this presence next to me, it was my actor soul mate, he was about forty. We had our arms around each other's waist (Fig 7). Another little boy jumped up on the urinal, he had dark hair and tanned skin. The actor and me looked at the stained glass windows. The two little boys were holding hands and smiling down at us. The urinals parted in the middle and sank to the ground. We walked through to this blue sand, and my soul mate and I became one.

Here we see the sacred urinals together with the true masculinity, sealed in the elemental blue, chained and yet free, in the gold of the higher personality in his name letter. Here we see also in a *coniunctio* drama the two divine boys with the alter ego, the actor soul mate, in which the true masculinity is manifest, from the intensity of the excrement to the harmony of love on the warm sand.

Here we have, at the end of another dream, his return to the land of the urinals, to free the oppressed spirits chained in bondage from the past.

DREAM 11

I went in where the urinal was undulating in and out of the ground. The shadow figures cried out, 'help! we are trapped in here, we have been waiting for you to set us free'. I lit my lighter, there was no one there, the flame went out and I saw the shadowy figures again. I found a candle in a dustbin outside. I lit it and put it on the back of the undulating urinal, and started to pray. These men rose up through the floor, one of them said, 'you have prayed for us we are free'. The urinal collapsed into a heap. The men said, 'we will not forget, you remember that'. They shuffled out; they were dressed in Victorian poor shabby clothes. I said, 'you are dead, this is 1999'. They said, 'no, we have just begun life'. They thanked me and disappeared. I looked down; there was a soldier's button on the floor. A voice said, 'that is for you son'.

He seems to be commissioned as a warrior to set free, especially, an element of Victorian repression of sexuality that kept society in bondage. The undulating urinals are Freudian, alimentary and orgasmic.[17] In this and the previous dream they fall in a heap. From repentance in excrement the scene is lifted to the liberation of the soul, which we find in Jung.[18] This is effected through illumination and prayer and the lifting of the wider burden off the shoulders of the penitent through the power of the Cross, in which he wields a new priestly power that crystallises, symbolically, in the candle and his worship. The analysis goes on as he is led out to fulfil the vocation that his condition has placed him in, and which his experiences and dreams have developed. Like Prometheus he has been chained to the rocks, and the vultures of the Great Mother have almost destroyed the liver, but he survives to fight another day. It can be seen as a catalysed catharsis that reverses the power of accusing guilt into a healing wholeness and openness in purity that accepts and encounters.

7. CONCLUSION

The question arises, particularly in the popular consciousness where the norms of society have been fixed in a tradition for countless generations, as to a far wider understanding of the basis of gender orientation. In this context is incorporated the original paradisiacal state, and the Fall, as a blessed fault, is translated into the realm of the gods in a new wholeness, in which there is a progression towards a pleromatic completion.[19]

We can place some of this thought alongside our multiple gender syndrome, where the distortion of the fall from grace seems much more intense in the homosexual and lesbian instances and in the gender disphoric. The general attitudes of society and inbuilt conscience mechanisms of guilt, associated with normal sexuality, are intensified to the degree that the suffering and identity crises that result, marginalize these people from society into an almost ghetto situation. Any understanding of the basic nature of this situation, the distortion and perversion of which is common to all sexuality, has a potential for redemptive gain, an apotheosis, that puts the multiple kaleidoscopic process of a complex gender system, which partakes of the bill of debt to fate of heredity, into an evolutionary pattern where each succeeding generation complements the other. The understanding we have of mutation of acquired characteristics in the genotype makes a combination of meaningful coincidence[20] and lottery of chance into a complex question. But it also brings with it the realisation that, perhaps, these situations together with those whose fate it is to live them out, could enlighten mankind to a higher degree of understanding and consciousness of the basic patterns of meaning in our world.

It is relatively easy to hypostasise and make a bald statement such as the above, but we shall seek to put a foundation under our theory and argument and augment it with the facts of the analysis of our case, where a tangible process is still going on in terms of the physical and the psychological situation. Furthermore, we will examine multiple gender syndrome in history, where it is much more common, and appears more normal, than is apparent on the surface. Then we shall look at it in terms of new research and heredity in the genotype.

From the beginning in the fundamental archetypal pattern, born human under the curse of the law, there is a distortion of the origins. In the case under discussion, John takes on the new masculine sexuality syndrome and pays the price by being marginalized to the grass-roots in alcoholism and homosexuality, without the opportunity to realise his creative talent and abhorring the norms of work in society. Then there is the cirrhosis of the liver, the gall bladder operation, the enlarged omentum also operated on, the failure of the gender reorientation operation, and the hernia that is not only painful but distorts his self body image. In his creative talent, which cannot ultimately be blocked, there is an obsession with urinals – the mire and the shit. But in each of these situations there is a gradual process of redemption. The alcoholism is conquered, the creative talent finds the beginnings of an outlet, and the distended abdomen is being treated with partial success by a psychic surgeon. Through his dreams in analysis, he is learning to accept the distended abdomen as a creative principle, the pregnancy of the divine, psychological child. The obsession with the urinal is a basic Mercurial matrix which contains in itself the opposites and the excrement, in which the treasure can be found and the personality developed. Along with this redemption comes the seal of the divine approval, and a vocation. Here he takes on a priestly role to make real the awareness of the multiple gender syndrome, where there is catalysed the release of mankind from false guilt with the suffering and misunderstanding, to redemptive evolution in wholeness and fulfilment (see dreams 4, 5 and 11). We can see this in progression of the pictures, from the apotheosis of the urinals and the sacrifice of the phallus, to the head of a bird with lunar disc eyes, around which the uroboric serpent is tangled

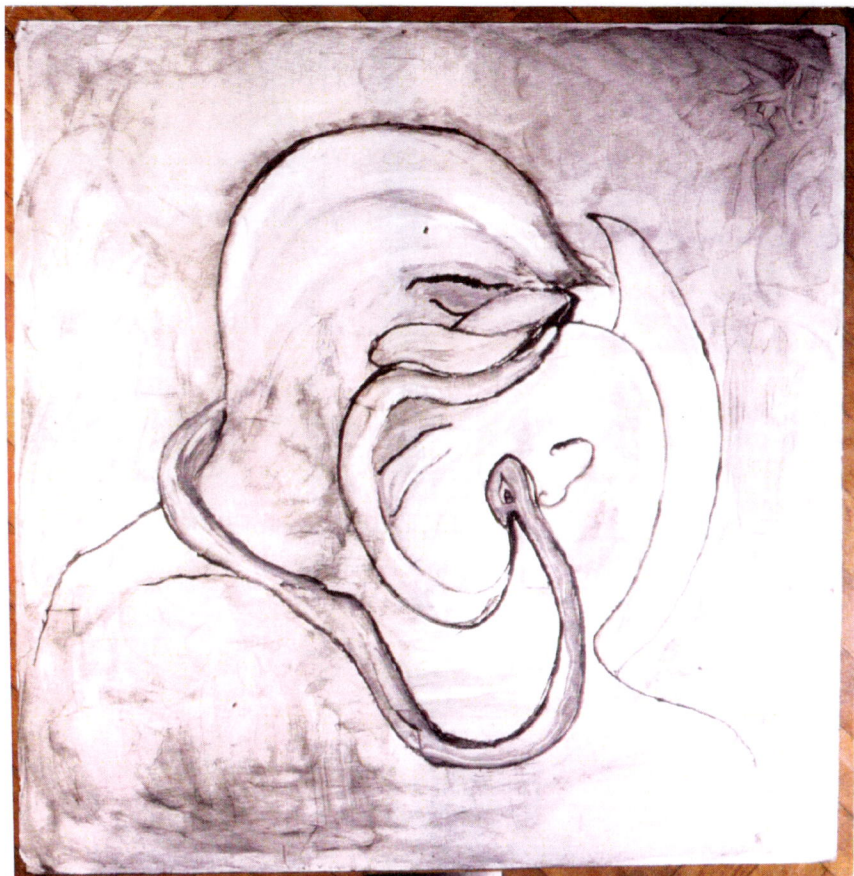

Figure 8. The *prima material* of the tangled instincts in the bird's head with lunar disc eyes and the uroboros with the scimitar as a dividing sword for healing transformation

and uncentred (Fig 8). The instincts from which the transformative renewal in the archetypes comes are there in the bird and serpent, but they suffer a distortion. The scimitar (outlined on the right) comes as the dividing sword of the logos, that threatens to cleave the soul of man into the fundamental divided schizophrenia between matter and spirit, and then heals and restores into a transformation of wholeness. But the next picture, in the progressive formation of the head, shows redeeming features of an archetypal order (Fig 9). It is encircled by a symmetrical untangled uroboros. The mouth is a

Figure 9. The redeeming head with the unentangled uroboros encircling the single pineal eye above the double eye of the opposites, which find their unity in the centre and circumference of the mouth of the new Self, incarnate in the body

Figure 10. Adam and the fruitful phallus of the tree of life
Miscellanea d'Alchimia (MS 15th century)

centre and a circle of the new wholeness of the self, a vortex of the void of
the beginning and a wholeness of the conjunction of the end. Between the
two eyes that look out in the existential opposites of life, the two that prefigure
the many, is the one pineal eye, the higher Self that sees into and creates the
final meaning.

Figure 11. The tree of life from the head of Eve and the skull of death and transformation Miscellanea d'Alchimia (MS., 14th cent.)

In other pictures we see the true hermaphrodite from which the complete masculinity arises. The Tree of Life in the phallus of Adam (Fig 10), coming out of the head of Eve (Fig 11), and in John's picture of the head of J'ai out of which grows the primal phallus (Fig 12). In this is constellated upon him a responsibility in vocation of this revelation (see dreams 4, 5 and 11), for it is as if he is consecrated with priestly power for world consciousness and discernment of meaning, particularly as mediated through the apotheosis of the gender dysphoric syndrome in the realisation of the Self in numinous symbol and image. In the existential situation there is a progression, in which the original primal archetypal engrams of the creation, which was very

Figure 12. The phallic head of J'ai, symbol of the personal tree of life, in apotheosis and transformation, and the union of masculine and feminine archetypal symbolic principles in earth and spirit

good, are evolving in a multiple gender syndrome in a redemptive, symbolic complex which puts a new light on creation. Perhaps we could talk about a 'creative redemption'. Furthermore, the complexity of the process is working towards a new and higher synthesis, from a basic thought that encompasses the original simplicity to one profoundly simple and obvious in itself. Wrought in the depths of despair, *de profundis*, the personality is redeemed in suffering, where the cross, as the transformative symbol of which there are many, is lifted up, and prefigures the resurrection (see above). If we look at the basic transformation there is translation in stages where the archetypal symbols come into their own, progression through the bodily to the psychological and the renewed archetypal in the spirit. We can find parallels in modern psychological understanding and in the alchemical schemas:

Psychological
1a. Ego bound state with feeble dominant.
2a. Ascent of the unconscious and/or descent of the ego into the unconscious.
3a. Conflict and synthesis of conscious and unconscious.
4a. Formation of a new dominant; circular symbols e.g. mandala, of the Self.

Alchemical
1b. Sick king enfeebled by age about to die.
2b. Disappearance of the king in his mother's body, or his dissolution in water.
3b. Pregnancy, sickbed symptoms, display of colours.
4b. King's son, hermaphrodite, rotundum.

In Our Case
1c. The nigredo, the mire.
2c. The near death of the old king in the depths of life amongst the urinals.
3c. The psychic pregnancy with the new transcendent symbols – the cross, the uroborus, the vortex at the centre of the circle.
4c. The union of the opposites, the monoculus or singular eye.

Moreover (4b), in the many coloured pictures we see the transforming

Mercurius, and the rotundum signifies the brain where the instincts are made whole in consciousness. Furthermore, there is integration between conscious and unconscious in the mandala (4a above). Then there is the apotheosis to the new hermaphrodite, where the alchemist of the *Rosarium Cruciformis*[21] goes further. Here, in the formation of his true masculinity through the acceptance of the feminine, we see the alchemical *filius regius* and queen luna, a syzygy (divine marriage) prefiguring the archetypal completion at the end of time. Here we see the importance, in the gender dysphoria that originally rejected the female body, of the reconciliation with the feminine principle, in our case in the archetypal dreams (1,2 & 3), before the complete transformation can take place. Through the integrating power of the feminine and the goddess, there comes the gradual movement from the dis-ease of the self image in the body, to the psychological, archetypal body beyond the merely physical, and eventually into an apotheosis of the whole personality.

Historically, if we go back to primitive society to the homosexuality of the warrior caste who, separated from the women, practised ritual sodomy that erects the phallus for penetration of the female, and sees in male friendship and brotherly love a normality of the homoerotic, we can extend this to the female relating to each other in order to relate to man. The knights of mediaeval times had their squires, which was not a sign of feminine degeneration but part of a noble masculinity. Mediaeval society, court and carnival, made use of all sorts of supposedly deformed creature; dwarfs and jesters, for instance, were used by the rulers to ridicule and confuse their enemies. In Elizabethan times, Shakespeare's plays abound with men playing women and women playing men. Today, the cult of transsexual, transvestite actors is prominent quite apart from the gay and lesbian scene. If we are proceeding to a multiracial society in a process of integration of complexes, then our society is building on a basic pattern of multiple gender that is increasing. With this comes a liberation of a high degree of creativity, and the enrichment of relationships in variations of eros, without the same biological insistence on procreation for the survival of the race.

We now come to the question of heredity. According to tradition the sins and righteousness of the fathers are continued in each successive generation. Jung points out that in a bill of debt to fate each generation has to compensate and balance the achievements and failures of the last. Hence the doctrines of heredity for the fathers' conduct of life. We get this in the Old Testament until in Jeremiah (31: 29-30), where it states that no longer will the fathers eat sour grapes and the children's teeth be set on edge, as each will be responsible for his own life. In an analysis of the unconscious we get a mixture of the two. The child inherits a responsibility to redeem the shortcomings of the parents, but also has its own individual task. In one sense each individual partakes of a collective responsibility for redemption in his share in world history, where 'no man is an island'. Where does this put the genotype, in particular in relation to the current researches? There is a hereditary pattern in the genes of infinite multiplicity. The individual must take on some of the characteristics not only of the race but also of the fathers, and there must at least in part be a pattern, synchronistically, of meaningful coincidence. Also, the process seems to obey the laws of chance like a gigantic lottery. But recent research shows positive mutations as being much more frequent than originally thought, which suggests the inheritance of acquired characteristics. Therefore, wherever there are genetic throw backs there must be a syndrome of evolution, in which, through creation and Fall, sins and righteousness, there is a progression, even if back and forth, regression for progression, of the human race. Furthermore, it is interesting to note that genes are not single but in pairs, and in the midst of this the male and female x and y chromosomes exist, dominant and recessive, in varying proportions. If the genotype is fundamental, here is a basis not only of the molecule male to female, but of the hermaphrodite in male and female homosexuals, and gender dysphoria in multiple combinations partaking of an archetypal norm.

It is interesting to note that although the Christ appears in the dreams as God and Son of God and puts a positive seal on the multiple gender syndrome, he also takes a role as suffering servant and as mediator, bringing forgiveness and encouragement and aiding self-determining independent action. Theologically, the Christ subordinates himself to the Father in the Godhead, and at his ascension says that his disciples will do greater works than he did. In our dreams there are figures of the priests who also affirm the pleasure of the gods (see Dream 5), as do the shadowy Mercurial figures of the Gnostic redeemer (see Dream 7). In this last we get affirmation of greater works and a higher revelation promised by the Christ (Jeremiah 14:12). The Christ as Son of Man recapitulates the works of mankind, and brings all things together in the Godhead at the final judgement.[22] The judgement here seems to be as to whether they, the dreamer and his alto ego, fulfil the chosen vocation in their distress, suffering and love, that is laid on them both by their situation and by the gods, to bring further emancipation and blessing on mankind. In the evolution of our understanding of the relationship between the sexes in civilisation and society, it has not been easily possible to comprehend the whole picture, which is contained in the teleological progression. The multiple gender syndrome has, we feel, a despised key role to play here in its Mercurial nature.

To round out the whole picture of multiple gender and its basis in archetypal principles, we must see that among body, psyche, and spirit there are not only creation and its concomitant archetypal constellations, but in the redemption of the evil in the opposites there is a dialogue between what is experienced in the body and what is experienced in the psyche. If you like, it is in the astral body that fulfilment of the process on the new archetypal level takes place, where, although the body is maimed and distorted in life, the psyche in those same gender combinations is potentially whole, and becoming increasingly whole in the spirit. In order to understand the process which is happening here, we must differentiate in our understanding between areas of bodily, psychic and spiritual existence. In the dreams there is a translation of the basic biological self to the psychic and spiritual spheres, which not only looks towards eternity but returns to the bodily world to achieve redemptive results.

Relating this to every department of life, we see here a fundamental theme running throughout as an Ariadne thread. The basic male and female projections as each other's other half, in animus and anima, become whole in the individuation process in an inner marriage (See **Schema (2)**), giving birth in themselves to the divine child of the Self. This child, for its development, suffers the Shadow conflict by being attacked by the raven devil, the negative principle, in order to develop to the great apotheosis of the archetypal hermaphrodite, incorporated in heredity to the great Tree of Life.[23] Male and male, and female and female too, have an inner marriage, both in themselves and in their animus and anima (See **Schema (2)**), and here the combinations begin to differentiate, vary, and become more complex. In the gender dysphoria the genes, although seeming to play tricks with body and soul, still produce, in their complexity, a definitely realisable synthesis to our understanding. Expanding this developing and redemptive spectrum can bring some bearing on the healing transformations that are inherent in the fundamental neurotic splits in the opposites, experienced in existential existence that we encounter in life. For instance, the paedophile is somewhere looking to relate to the lost child within that has been overlaid by the false adult, without which he cannot truly enter into the divine communion in himself and his environment. We cannot enter the Kingdom of God without the childlike state.[24] When the priest, in the course of his ministry, lays hands, and indeed his own soul, onto the dead soul to bring it back to life, in sacrament and spirit (as Elijah gave the kiss of life to the widow's son), it is a sacralisation of necrophilia. In this context we can see the fundamental law of evolving life, death and rebirth and, finally, death and resurrection.

8. THE REDEMPTIVE SYNDROME AND THE WORK OF GOD

It might seem to some readers that this is an isolated case, an eccentric one-off of a perverted hybrid cast-off from society, and an aberration that had no purpose or meaning except as a riddle, an unsolvable question mark. But we would like to emphasise that this is not an isolated case, but a thread that runs through the collective unconscious in the dreams of men and women, and is acted out in the lives of creative people and people of genius, who themselves had to stand out from the misjudgement of a society that is not ready for their contribution. We quote here the dream of a film director (straight heterosexual) who is training in analysis, as preliminary reinforcement of our position.

DREAM 12
I am at the beach with surfer friends in France. I meet a young-thirties woman wearing a bikini, with long blonde hair, olive skin, and a voluptuous athletic body. We talk and there is an instant connection. The conversation evolves curiously in that she begins to talk to me telepathically. At first I am unsure that that which I am experiencing is real, and unsure about how to use my psychic tools to talk back. She speaks again and guides me to use my mind to speak, and in very little time we are talking in our minds comfortably. We turn away from each other and look out to sea, and continue to talk and get to know each other. She asks me if I would like to slip away with her for an hour or so. She guarantees me that we won't be missed. We drive to a nearby house.

Once in the house we continue to talk in our minds, and she says she would like to make love to me. I agree. She takes off her bikini top seductively, and she registers in her mind that I like what I see. She takes off her bottoms and I notice that she has a penis. She is a hermaphrodite. I am conscious of my own non-averse reaction. If anything, I am curious in my attitude. We embrace and I explore her sex with my fingers, and find that behind her erect penis she has a moist vagina. I register the peculiarity of what my senses are discovering. We make love, and as I give her pleasure we continue our psychic dialogue, whereby she communicates what she likes and how she likes it, effortlessly. Then follows a combination of making love to her and being made love to by her, of penetrating and being penetrated. There is a sense of abandonment to the coitus, paralleled with the ascending pleasure being registered in each other's minds simultaneously. The pleasure builds to a point of mutual orgasm, that is one like I have never experienced before. A combined orgasm that we both register psychically, an explosion in both of our minds, at the same time as it is also experienced by the other. Four orgasms as it were. Soon afterwards I feel a massive surge of love for her, and I see that she has felt it for me too.

We return to the beach. She goes as she came. I return to my friends, and my girlfriend appears on the beach to call us all to go home and eat.

This shows that the gender dysphoric syndrome in the hermaphrodite is experienced in the dreams of straight people.

Early in the 20th century there emerged the *pissetières* of Paris, and in particular the writings of Marcel Proust and Henry Miller. Miller wrote about them a great deal, and how, almost in tears, he would go to the dilapidated urinals in the rue St. Jacques where, in the evening, the gas lamps on the streets would light up and so would the lights on the urinals. A strange ritual would take place in the 'chapels', as the urinals were popularly called, of Greek love and men lost in torment of their own conflict. The loneliness and anonymity in the darkness of these men was of paramount importance and an essential requirement in the ghetto situation, where their activities and rituals were a part of the fabric of Parisian life at that time. Proust saw darkness as having the effect of eliminating the first stage of pleasure, the fear and negative transference in the erotic encounter, and allowing entry straightaway into the world of caress. All the old habits fall away. Hands, lips, bodies make contact immediately in this response of the body that does not withdraw but approaches, and gives an unprejudiced notion of the person. Proust was on the front line in talking about the shadow world of the homosexuals in an ironic way. The Baron de Charles was a frequent visitor to these urinals. Henry Miller is quoted as saying: 'How can a Frenchman know, that one of the first things that strikes the eye of a visiting American, which moves him and warms his guts, is this omnipresent urinal.'

It seems that in every decade the urinal has figured in literature and art. It continues in a piece written by Johnny Blue, which he called *De Profundis* – 'Out of the Depths', mainly in his own words but with quotations from extensive writings. In his own words:

My pictures depict my urinals as confessionals, as a way of coming to terms with the angst and shadow in relation to religion and guilt, sin and forgiveness. The idea of ritual cleansing in a urinal appeals to me greatly as a form of prayer out of the depths of my own darkness, to be performed with candles and with incense, to be offered unto God as a way of saying, 'here I stand in one of life's lowest denominators, amid the stench and waste of the bladders of men, praying to be transformed in spirit'. The urinal cleansing I have in mind has no blasphemous intent.

The acceptance of such a ritual, primarily in the heart, makes a sacrificial altar within where a cleansing of the very birth *inter urinam et faeces* takes place, and where the divine, secret treasure is found. In the transformation of the ritual is a cleansing which, in its Mercurial nature, throws light and redemption upon a sick situation, and has its contribution to a higher discernment of the gender situation in its multiple opposites. Here the archetypes reveal their basic structure and interaction to heal the frustrations and torments of guilt and accusations of perversion, that beset the scapegoats of our world. He continues:

So to perform such a ritual within the urinal symbol would, for me, be the way I would choose to do this. Like all true rituals, it collectively goes out from its centre, like ripples in a pond, to all whom it may touch, quicken and heal. It would be a way of laying the ghosts of being drawn into urinals. It has taken me years to understand this, but now I do. Some might say I have been influenced by dark forces to write this, but how can those who have not known darkness, know light? This is why I have written this story. If we stay in the darkness only, we are lost. But if we seek the light in the darkness, we will find our way out of the abyss. The fascination of being drawn to the brick walls and tiles of the urinals seems now to make sense. It is not an obsession. It is a fact of life that our perception of things, and the world around us, can sometimes yield symbolic meaning for the complexities of our natures.

There are many creative people (philosophers, actors, playwrights, sculptors, dancers, artists) strolling on Hampstead Heath in order to come to terms with, or to understand, their own existence. I am one of them. I don't say they all find the urinals as a catalyst for the understanding of their conflicts as I do, where I am not obsessed. The conflicts which I meet in that shadowy world are reflected back to me, which in turn helps me to gain insight, in my person, of the human condition and its feelings of futility. Colin Wilson, in *The Outsider*, writes of a person nauseated by his own being and by the whole of his existence. This idea of being nauseated mirrors my own compulsion to experience the dark, cold, malodorous hollowness of old urinals which now, I hope, are becoming extinct, yet in my heart have become shrines of transformation, and containers of the treasure hard to attain. Is it to do with my gender dysphoria? The answer first to that is, no. It is a far more deeply rooted, causeless cause, which I cannot reach. I can only scratch the surface and touch it through its symbols. And yet the gender situation is part of it, for, paradoxically, where it complicates the situation it also throws light on a Transformative situation.

These are the Mercurial transformations that the Gnostic redeemer has been joining to the Christian redemption, which has already been spoken about.

Somehow, in the ritualisation of, and my need to see, the urinals as cleansing altars of transformation, I feel I bear the conflict of generations, past and present, at the altars of the archetypes. Christ and the gods accept these as offerings for the redemptive understanding in our world.

Something of the redemptive conflict is expressed in his own version of two Psalms:

Psalm 35
Let not the accuser, harbinger of self-attack, negative thoughts and paranoia,
Hold power over me and gloat at my torment and downfall.
Let not the accuser, falsifier of truths, point his barbed finger into my mind without reason,

Save that of his own downfall and the release of the demons that devour me.

Psalm 56
Be merciful unto me O God, for demons hotly pursue me.
All day long they press their attack.
They are slanderous, filling my soul with anguish,
My mind with paranoia, self-hate and guilt,
To swell their own pride.
Their freedom, my frustration and conflict,
Have mercy on me O God. As I seek thee,
And in my seeking I wander through the shadow world,
Preserve me and raise them up at the appointed time.

The work which is done with our own neuroses, diseases and imperfections is part of the opus of the evolving world soul. It is the work of the alchemist, the Gnostic, the Christian, and the central experience of all religions.

Here, as we follow our argument, is a basic archetypal pattern in which, as well as as in spite of the fallen nature of man in the redemptive understanding of the multiple gender syndrome, there emerges a natural and wholesome feeling for gender orientation, so often decimated by guilt, inferiority and persecution.

9. SUMMARY

We can hypostasise and cautiously affirm in what we have here shown as a psychological picture of gender orientation, particularly as it completes its fullness in gender dysphoria, that the Mercurial nature of gender dysphoria is a key catalyst in archetypal evolution. It can even alter our perspective of narrow legalistic taboos that stultify the relating power of eros. This has profound implications for the understanding of our culture and its working out in our way of life, and the implied judgment of our society on our fellow human beings. It could be said to be putting a new face on humankind in our world, and also putting a new face on the God image.[25] This God, in creating the divine spark in the world and in humanity, manifests a reproductive process through the archetypes of the Father God and Mother Goddess. This is universal to the many great creation myths. In so doing this God identifies with created humanity and, therefore, humanity has a place in the life of the Godhead which is incomplete without it.[26] This gives a more complete spectrum to our discernment of the dynamics of the psyche. Here dysphorics can find redemptive harmony, peace and meaning in the service of man, woman, child, the soul, God himself and the archetypal gods.

It might be helpful in clearing up any possible misunderstandings to see in what sense the enigmatic figure of the Christ appears in our presentation of the theme. Throughout, wherever in doctrine Christ is Son of God and Son of Man there is an intermediate position in which he appears as an archetype of the Self, the mediatory principle between God and man and in the Anthropos, the God Man. As a synthesis of the Christ event and the Mercurial Gnostic redeemer, he comes as a function of man made in the image of God, that brings God and man, evolving together and mutually redeeming, as one of the great principles of the syzygy of the hermaphrodite in the divine marriage.[27] It also puts it in the realm of human psychology including its numinous and evolving nature. This can be seen as the emergence of the individuating Self as a priestly figure in the divine opus with a reciprocal function for both man and God, in which there is redemptive meaning in the perplexity, misunderstandings and suffering in our world (see dreams 4, 5 and 11).

Note: The term 'God/Man' implies mankind as man and woman, and God as Father God and Mother Goddess, united in the great hermaphrodite of the Self, the Jungian and Gnostic Self, seen in the apocalyptic Son of Man in Medieval Christianity.

APPENDIX I

We passed over the question of persons that had normal physical relationships, and often children of the union who also, either in separate times of life or simultaneously, sustained physical erotic relationships with both sexes. In particular we stated that they should be regarded as completely separate syndromes, because at that stage we were primarily basing our argument on a case of gender dysphoria where, to all practical purposes, the separation would really be the only way of looking at it. But there is the case of parallel male-to-female, and homosexual and lesbian relationships. This would appear to be more normal than at first sight. If we start with our basic premise of the hermaphrodite, it would appear that it would be completely normal for each individual to have erotic transferences both heterosexually and to the same sex. In adolescence, the homosexual and lesbian stages in erotic transference are perfectly normal and more usually experienced than not, and in themselves can be preliminary in enhancing the heterosexual relationship, as we have previously explained. What could be more natural where eros is the relating factor and the basis of friendship between man and woman, man and man, and woman and woman than, as well as basic heterosexual union in a highly libidinous man or woman, there should also be homoerotic transferences that could be mutually satisfied in physical as well as merely psychological relationships, that are deep, free, fulfilling and even spiritual.

But this also has a deeper and important significance in our syndrome in the individuation process. Animus and anima respectively, projected and introjected, bring about an inner marriage and a whole person not at the mercy of unconscious projection. If we have individuated persons brought together in this way, in respect of their inner hemaphroditic marriage there are various combinations, as we see in our **Schema (3)** below, in which the gender orientation can combine in relationship in a whole and wholesome balanced way:

F　　　　　M
normal　↘ ↗ homosexual
biological　　M
anima ←——→ animus
hermaphrodite

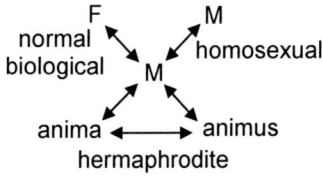

Mutually projected on male
and female in which they
are united in himself

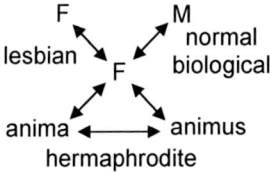

F　　　　　M
　　↘ ↗ normal
lesbian　F　biological
anima ←——→ animus
hermaphrodite

Mutually projected on male
and female in which they
are united in herself

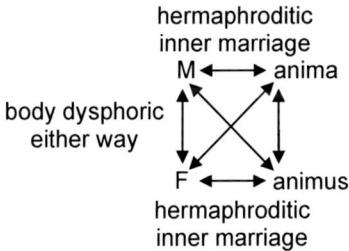

hermaphroditic
inner marriage
M ←——→ anima
body dysphoric
either way
F ←——→ animus
hermaphroditic
inner marriage

Mutual inter-reaction conscious
without being at the mercy of
the unconscious projection

For integrated individuals it would seem a logical conclusion that this could naturally happen. It does not take much imagination to see that there are a very large number of different combinations that can proliferate out, and which can serve to facilitate a total relationship to persons and environment on a universal level through the freeing of the basic eros.

If we now turn to gender dysphoria we have a more complicated picture. (Physical as opposed to psychological consummation is not a simple issue here, but on looking into it appears, especially in the psyche, as a special case which actually throws a great deal of light on our understanding of the multiple gender syndrome.) From a psychological point of view in particular if at first sight rather awkward, it can be thought of as seminal to our hypothesis.

To see this we have said that multiple gender has its basis in the archetypes of creation which, through redemption and re-creation, is evolving to a new fulfilment in a higher synthesis, in which the beginning and the end are one progressing through all levels of the archetypal symbol of marriage. This goes from a simple postulate through every complexity of existence, and resolves in a basic simplicity of principle, as we shall continue to argue. But the creation is not only simple, *exnihilo* in male and female archetypes, but in this splitting into opposites there is the descent of Mercurius into the world as an agent of creation. Mercurius contains all the opposites and is a complex trickster, and the creation of the gender dysphoric is primarily of Mercurius. This Mercurius is the matrix of the existential situation in which human kind finds itself and naturally evolves. Therefore, through psychological death and rebirth to transformation, we can argue that the gender dysphoric throws light on this Mercurial syndrome of redemptive evolution, and is part of the very substance of this reactive process.

To look at this from a wider viewpoint, the multiple gender syndrome can be parallelled in the doctrine of the one and the many, where the singularity of the individual through the primary dual hermaphrodite splits into any amount of complexes that, kaleidoscopically, break and remake to evolve around the one in infinite multiplication to form the Self. This is certainly true of the one-and-the-many Hindu and Eastern world. But if we look at our syndrome from the point of view of the West, it is interesting to see that our complexes take the shape of the Gnostic axiom of Maria Prophetessa.[28] This axiom, $1+2+3+4=10$, is an incorporated formula applied, firstly, into the split in God and man (1 & 2 above), implied in creation and the fall from grace. This is followed by a redemptive trinitarium and quaternity principle (3 & 4 above) of a masculine godhead related to the feminine, which includes the Earth and humanity. This progresses to the denarius (10 above), the principle of infinite multiplication which in Alchemy is known as the 'multiplicatio'.

APPENDIX II

To recapitulate and bring our argument together, here in our multiple gender syndrome we see the straightforward heterosexual relationships and, logically through the hermaphrodite, the relatively straightforward homoerotic and bisexual relationships. But in the gender dysphoric there is the relatively more complex Mercurial trickster element which, through creation and the Fall, gives rise to the Gnostic redeemer. *This is the real focus of the process of redemption for both God and mankind, where the opposites are united through the mercurial as well as the single, simple creation into a new evolving wholeness.* This, in the existential situation, gives the gender dysphoric a key role in our understanding of the basic nature of mankind, as it is created and evolving, where the despised and marginalized element is the matrix of a reaction, and where, in the opposites of existence, the evil and the good, the darkness and the light, the suffering and glory, etc., of humanity, are brought into a synthesis of realisation. We can understand that in its very trickster-hermetic element, there is contained a wisdom that is key to the *coincidentia oppositorum* of the pleroma as the final fulfilment at the end of time, where the dark and light side of God become one in the true consummation of all things, and where every category of existence will be gathered into one in a completion in transformation.[29] This, if we follow it in the life situation and in the psyche, somehow strikingly comes over, not necessarily in completion but in a progression that gives us some clues as to a greater understanding of the morality of the sexual situation, as well as in multiple kaleidoscopic and symbolic processes in which all aspects of existence are included. Here in the multiple, archetypal gender syndrome there is called for a radical readjustment in our attitudes and in the care of the soul, both pastoral and therapeutic, towards the normal, homoerotic, lesbian and dysphoric personalities where a narrow moralistic censor is responsible for much of the suffering, guilt and fear that is incurred through a false conscience and projection of society's own shadow. Here is the potential to redeem a curse that decimates both the individual and our culture. With this can come the restoration of a category of wholeness, balanced and normal personality, to play its part in the longed for alleviation and cure of the sickness of the soul of our world. This has the potential of a progression to a whole, balanced personality that, in itself and all it has been through, has a role to redeem our world society through the understanding and culture in each individual and group that carries a differing multiple gender orientation. It partakes in the central experience of life in a symbol of marriage – the coming together of opposites in matter, body, soul and spirit. There the principle of original simplicity traverses every conceivable experience in its complexity, and resolves again into a simple principle that restores the true unity and harmony that is inherent in the beginning as well as the end. A process in which, we humbly hope, our case and the argument stemming from it may dispel, and alleviate, some of the ignorance and misunderstanding surrounding the multiple gender syndrome.

APPENDIX III

This is not just a theoretical hypothesis but based on living experience. This includes the conflict, wound and suffering inherent in the first sexual encounter, particularly in the homosexual and gender-dysphoric, where fear and anxiety distort healthy, loving relationships in depth.

NOTES

1 Jung, C.G. CW11, *Answer to Job.*

2 Gender Dysphoria – when an individual has differing physical and psychological gender orientation, i.e., a male physically may feel and act sexually female, correspondingly, a female physically may identify with the male.

3 The word 'soul' as used here stands for the inner person or spirit, which expresses itself in symbolic images projected beyond the body.

4 These images are archetypes which are the complement of the bodily hermaphrodite, which emerges as the soul develops, and unite in the psyche beyond the body to form the divine child of the Self.

5 This is the psychological conception of the Self, the greater true man, which is the reunion of the opposites. See Jung, C.G. CW16 *The Psychology of the Transference.*

6 Enantiodromia – a change in the dynamics of the soul; usually a complete reversal of complexes and opposites, which often includes synthesis and transformation.

7 Jung, C.G. CW14, *Mysterium Coniunctionis*, paras. 109-110.

8 As we have seen in the dreams, his negative psycho/physical relationship to the feminine had to be, to some degree, healed and integrated for a stable masculinity.

9 Michael Fordham, known for his work on the individuation process in the child and personality development, writes of (original) integration, deintegration, and reintegration.

10 After the Fall from paradise, with its loss and potential gain in consciousness as 'gods knowing good and evil', the existential condition of life between the opposites has its wound and conflict where, in between the tension, there emerges a *tertium non datur* – a reconciling, transcendent symbol of the central experience. In the West this is predominantly the mediatory Christ/Self – the blessed fault that man should sin that Christ should come, which restores the original wholeness. This then develops a new synthesis that incorporates the existential gain and leads to a new Self, evolving in the individual and collective – the world soul.

11 Ibid.

12 Ibid.

13 Meister Eckehart and Angelus Silesius. CW16, *Psychological Types*, paras 407-433.

14 The serpent of nature evolves into the serpent of wisdom, of healing – the caduceus – to the crucified serpent as the redeeming symbol.

15 'Out of Egypt have I called my Son.' The Israelites in bondage in Egypt are led out to the freedom of the promised land, where the doctrines of the Judaeo-Christian redeemer-god principle develop out of the Egyptian pantheon – from the sins of the flesh to the quickening of the spirit, and their integration in the word made flesh.

16 Jung, C.G. CW14, *Mysterium Coniunctionis,* Plates 8-9. The archetypal spectrum

of the symbols and images in their realisation through the instincts, are often seen in multiple colours as in refracted light, between the infra red and the ultra violet.

17 The Freudian elements of psyche in the body progress, in Jung, to symbols of the archetypal complexes in matter, body, psyche and spirit, in an understanding of a wider, holistic synthesis in the progressive journey of the soul, in multiple transformations.

18 Ibid.

19 See above pp.31 and 50, and notes 9, 10, 11 and 28.

20 Jung, whilst acknowledging that at certain levels there were causal connections to the reactions between certain nuclear complexes in the psyche, postulated that there was a groundswell of archetypal symbolic complexes, that without logical interaction nevertheless spontaneously constellated, yet not purely at random but reacting together in terms of a *meaningful coincidence*. This principle of an underlying, unseen intelligence he called *synchronicity* (See also pp.10 and 38).

21 Jung, C.G. CW16, *The Practice of Psychotherapy*, 'The Psychology of the Transference'.

22 I Peter 4:5

23 Jung, C.G. CW16, ibid.,Chs. 9 & 10.

24 Mark 10:15, and Luke 18:17.

25 Jung, C.G. CW11, *Psychology and Religion*, 'Answer to Job'.

26 Ibid.

27 Jung, C.G. CW16, ibid., Ch.10, fig 10.

28 The axiom of Maria Prophetessa is a leitmotif running throughout Gnosticism that has many inexhaustible angles, but throws a certain light on the multiple gender syndrome.

29 Revelation, 21:1-7.